COMPREHENSIVE ROAD MAP TO CONTENT MARKETING AND SEO

Your Extensive Visibility Guide To Boosting Your Business Online Alongside Driving Traffic For Your Site.

BY

DARRYL ROJAS

Copyright Notice

© 2024 DARRYL ROJAS. All rights reserved. This document and its contents are copyrighted by Darryl Rojas. No part of this document may be reproduced, stored, or transmitted in any form or by any means, electronic, mechanical, photocopying, recording, or otherwise, without the prior written permission of Darryl Rojas.

TABLE OF CONTENTS

INTRODUCTION TO "Content Marketing and SEO" 10

CHAPTER 1 11

    IMPORTANCE OF CONTENT MARKETING AND SEO 11

CHAPTER 2 17

    UNDERSTANDING CONTENT MARKETING 17

CHAPTER 3 23

    DEVELOPING A CONTENT MARKETING STRATEGY 23
        Content Marketing Funnel 27

CHAPTER 4 30

    CONTENT PLANNING AND IDEATION 30

CHAPTER 5 40

    CREATING HIGH-QUALITY CONTENT 40

PART 2: SEO Essentials..........................48

CHAPTER 6..49

INTRODUCTION TO SEO.................................49
What is SEO and Why It Matters.................... 49

CHAPTER 7..57

    KEYWORD RESEARCH............................... 57

CHAPTER 8..67

    ON-PAGE SEO... 67
    Optimizing Titles and Meta Descriptions......... 67

CHAPTER 9..76

    TECHNICAL SEO..76
    Website Speed and Performance................... 76

PART 3: Integrating Content Marketing and SEO 84

CHAPTER 10..85

    CONTENT OPTIMIZATION FOR SEO........... 85

CHAPTER 11..93
    LINK BUILDING AND BACKLINKS.............. 93

Importance of Backlinks...................93

CHAPTER 12.......................................**101**

CONTENT DISTRIBUTION AND PROMOTION 102
SOCIAL MEDIA MARKETING...................... 102
PAID ADVERTISING......................................107

PART 4: Advanced Strategies and Tools........ 110

CHAPTER 13.......................................**111**

ADVANCED SEO TECHNIQUES..................111
SCHEMA MARKUP AND STRUCTURED DATA 111
LOCAL SEO STRATEGIES........................... 114
VOICE SEARCH OPTIMIZATION................. 117

CHAPTER 14.......................................**122**

CONTENT MARKETING AUTOMATION.....122
WORKFLOW AUTOMATION......................... 124

CHAPTER 15.......................................**128**

ANALYTICS AND PERFORMANCE MEASUREMENT..**128**
Key Metrics to Track...................................... 129
Tools for Monitoring and Analyzing

Performance..131
Using Data to Refine Your Strategy..............134

Part 5: Case Studies and Real-World

Applications.. **136**

CHAPTER 16..**136**

SUCCESSFUL CONTENT MARKETING AND SEO CASE STUDIES...................................137
LESSONS LEARNED FROM TOP BRANDS.....139

CHAPTER 17..**144**

ISSUES AND REMEDIES IN SEO AND CONTENT MARKETING.............................. **144**
PRACTICAL SOLUTIONS AND BEST PRACTICES..147
FUTURE TRENDS IN CONTENT MARKETING AND SEO.. 150

CHAPTER 18..**152**

BRINGING IT ALL TOGETHER................... **152**
Recap of Key Points...153
FINAL TIPS AND RECOMMENDATIONS... 162
ENCOURAGEMENT FOR CONTINUED LEARNING AND EXPERIMENTATION....... 164
CONCLUSION...**165**

INTRODUCTION TO "Content Marketing and SEO"

Welcome to "Content Marketing and SEO," a comprehensive guide designed to help you navigate the dynamic landscape of digital marketing. Whether you're a seasoned marketer looking to refine your strategy or a beginner eager to learn the ropes, this book offers valuable insights and practical advice to enhance your content marketing and SEO efforts.

CHAPTER 1

IMPORTANCE OF CONTENT MARKETING AND SEO

In today's digital age, content marketing and SEO are more crucial than ever. High-quality content serves as the backbone of your online presence, attracting and engaging your target audience while building brand authority and trust. Simultaneously, SEO ensures that your content is discoverable by search engines, driving organic traffic to your website and increasing visibility.

Effective content marketing allows you to connect with your audience on a deeper level, providing value through informative, entertaining, and relevant content. SEO complements this by optimizing your content to meet search engine algorithms' requirements, ensuring that your efforts reach the widest possible audience. Together, these strategies create a powerful synergy, enhancing your online presence and driving sustainable growth.

Overview of the Book

This book is divided into five parts, each focusing on a critical aspect of content marketing and SEO. We'll start with the basics, building a strong foundation before moving into more advanced techniques and real-world applications. Here is a little peek at what to expect:

1. **Foundations of Content Marketing**: We'll begin by exploring the fundamentals of content marketing, from understanding its definition and evolution to developing a robust content strategy. You'll learn about content planning, ideation, and how to create high-quality content that resonates with your audience.

2. **SEO Essentials**: Next, we'll dive into the world of SEO. You'll discover how search engines work, the importance of keyword research, and the intricacies of on-page and technical SEO. This section provides the essential knowledge needed to optimize your content effectively.

3. **Integrating Content Marketing and SEO**: Once you have a solid grasp of content marketing and SEO basics, we'll explore how to integrate these strategies seamlessly. You'll learn about content optimization, link building, and effective content distribution and promotion techniques.

4. **Advanced Strategies and Tools**: This section covers advanced SEO techniques, content marketing automation, and the importance of analytics. We'll discuss tools and strategies to help you stay ahead in the ever-evolving digital landscape.

5. **Case Studies and Real-World Applications**: Finally, we'll look at successful content marketing and SEO campaigns, common challenges, and practical solutions. You'll gain insights from real-world examples and learn how to apply these lessons to your own strategy.

What You Will Learn

By the end of this book, you will have a comprehensive understanding of both content marketing and SEO. Specifically, you will learn:

1. **The Essentials of Content Marketing**: Understand what content marketing is, its evolution, and the key benefits it offers. You'll discover various types of content marketing and how to leverage them to meet your goals.

2. **Creating and Implementing a Content Strategy**: Learn how to set clear goals, identify your target audience, and develop a content marketing funnel. We'll guide you through the process of content planning, ideation, and creation, ensuring you can produce high-quality content consistently.

3. **SEO Fundamentals and Techniques**: Gain a solid understanding of SEO, including keyword research, on-page optimization, and technical SEO. You'll learn how to optimize your content to improve its search engine ranking and drive organic traffic.

4. **Integrating Strategies for Maximum Impact**: Discover how to optimize your content for SEO, build high-quality backlinks, and effectively distribute and promote your content. You'll learn to create a cohesive strategy that maximizes your efforts' impact.

5. **Advanced Strategies and Performance Measurement**: Explore advanced SEO techniques, automation tools, and analytics. You'll learn how to measure your performance, analyze data, and refine your strategy for continuous improvement.

6. **Real-World Applications and Case Studies**: Benefit from practical insights and lessons learned from successful campaigns. You'll be equipped to overcome common challenges and stay ahead of industry trends.

As you embark on this journey through "Content Marketing and SEO," you'll gain the knowledge and skills needed to create a powerful digital marketing strategy. Let's get started and unlock the full potential of your content and SEO efforts!

PART 1: FOUNDATIONS OF CONTENT MARKETING

CHAPTER 2

UNDERSTANDING CONTENT MARKETING

In this chapter, we'll dive into the world of content marketing, exploring its definition, evolution, key benefits, and various types. Understanding these fundamentals will provide you with a solid foundation to build your content marketing strategy.

DEFINITION AND EVOLUTION

DEFINITION: A strategic marketing approach, content marketing aims to attract and retain a well-defined audience by producing and disseminating valuable, pertinent, and consistent content. In the end, the ultimate goal is to encourage profitable customer action. Unlike traditional advertising, which interrupts the audience with promotional messages, content marketing aims to provide genuinely useful information that solves problems, answers questions, or entertains, thereby building trust and loyalty over time.

EVOLUTION: The concept of content marketing isn't new; it has been around for centuries in various forms.

One of the earliest examples dates back to 1895, when John Deere published "The Furrow," a magazine providing farmers with tips and advice. This was a pioneering effort to build a relationship with customers through valuable content rather than direct product promotion.

Over the years, content marketing has evolved significantly with the rise of digital media. The internet has opened up new opportunities for content distribution and audience engagement. Social media platforms, blogs, podcasts, videos, and other digital formats have become integral to content marketing strategies. Today, brands use sophisticated data analytics to understand audience preferences and tailor their content to meet specific needs and behaviors.

Key Benefits of Content Marketing

Content marketing offers numerous benefits that make it an essential component of any modern marketing strategy. The following are some of the main benefits:

1. **Builds Brand Awareness**: By consistently producing high-quality content, you can increase your brand's visibility and reach. When your content is shared across various channels, it helps more people become aware of your brand.

2. **Establishes Authority and Trust**: Providing valuable information positions your brand as an expert in your industry. When you educate your audience and help them solve problems, they are more likely to trust your brand and see you as a credible source.

3. **Engages and Retains Customers**: Engaging content keeps your audience interested and coming back for more. By creating a relationship through consistent communication, you can increase customer loyalty and retention.

4. **Supports SEO Efforts**: High-quality, relevant content improves your search engine rankings. When your content answers questions that people are searching for, search engines recognize this and rank your site higher in search results, driving organic traffic to your site.

5. **Generates Leads and Conversions**: Content marketing helps attract potential customers and guide them through the buying process. By offering valuable content at different stages of the customer journey, you can nurture leads and encourage conversions.

6. **Cost-Effective**: Compared to traditional advertising methods, content marketing is often more cost-effective. Creating and distributing content can be done with relatively low investment, and the long-term benefits can be substantial.

Types of Content Marketing

There are various types of content marketing, each with its own unique benefits and best practices. These are a few of the most common categories, summarized here:

1. **Blog Posts**: Blogs are one of the most common forms of content marketing. They allow you to share in-depth information, provide value to your audience, and improve your website's SEO. Regularly updated blogs can position your brand as an industry authority and keep your audience engaged.

2. **Videos**: Video content is highly engaging and can be used to explain complex concepts, showcase products, or tell stories. Platforms like YouTube, Vimeo, and social media make it easy to share video content with a broad audience.

3. **Infographics**: Infographics combine visuals and text to present information in a clear, concise, and engaging way. They are highly shareable and can help simplify complex data, making it easier for your audience to understand and remember.

4. **Ebooks and Whitepapers**: These in-depth resources provide detailed information on specific topics and can be used to generate leads by offering them in exchange for contact information. They demonstrate your expertise and provide substantial value to your audience.

5. **Podcasts**: Podcasts are a popular way to reach audiences who prefer audio content. They allow you to discuss industry topics, interview experts, and provide valuable insights in a format that listeners can enjoy on the go.

6. **Social Media Posts**: Social media platforms are essential for distributing content and engaging with your audience. Short, impactful posts can drive traffic to your website, promote your content, and foster community interaction.

7. **Case Studies**: Case studies showcase real-life examples of how your products or services have helped customers achieve their goals. They provide social proof and can be highly persuasive in demonstrating the value of your offerings.

8. **Email Newsletters**: Email marketing allows you to deliver personalized content directly to your audience's inbox. Regular newsletters can keep your audience informed, engaged, and connected to your brand.

9. **Webinars and Live Streams**: These interactive formats allow you to engage with your audience in real-time, providing value through live demonstrations, Q&A sessions, and in-depth discussions.

Understanding content marketing's definition, evolution, benefits, and types equips you with the knowledge to create a successful strategy. As we move into the next chapter, we'll explore how to develop a content marketing strategy that aligns with your goals and resonates with your target audience.

CHAPTER 3

DEVELOPING A CONTENT MARKETING STRATEGY

Creating a successful content marketing strategy is crucial to achieving your marketing goals and engaging your target audience. In this chapter, we'll explore how to set clear goals and objectives, identify your target audience, and develop a content marketing funnel that guides your audience from awareness to conversion.

Setting Goals and Objectives

The first step in developing a content marketing strategy is to establish clear, measurable goals and objectives. These will guide your efforts and provide a benchmark for evaluating your success. Here's how to create goals and objectives that work:

1. **Define Your Overall Business Goals**: Start by understanding your broader business objectives. Are you trying to enhance client retention, raise revenue, create leads, or raise brand awareness? Align your content marketing goals with these overarching business goals to ensure that your efforts contribute to the bigger picture.

2. **Set Specific, Measurable Goals**: Vague goals like "increase traffic" or "boost engagement" are difficult to measure. Instead, set specific, quantifiable goals. For example, "increase website traffic by 20% in the next six months" or "generate 50 new leads per month." Specific goals help you track progress and make data-driven decisions.

3. **Establish Key Performance Indicators (KPIs)**: KPIs are metrics that help you measure your progress toward your goals. Common content marketing KPIs include website traffic, social media engagement, lead generation, conversion rates, and customer retention. Choose KPIs that align with your goals and regularly monitor them to gauge your success.

4. **Set Realistic and Achievable Objectives**: While it's important to aim high, setting unrealistic goals can lead to frustration and burnout. Ensure that your objectives are attainable given your resources, budget, and timeframe. Consider using the SMART criteria (Specific, Measurable, Achievable, Relevant, Time-bound) to set effective objectives.

5. **Prioritize Your Goals**: If you have multiple goals, prioritize them based on their importance to your business. Assign resources appropriately and concentrate

on the objectives that will have the biggest impact. This helps you maintain a clear direction and avoid spreading your efforts too thin.

Identifying Your Target Audience

Understanding your target audience is essential for creating content that resonates and drives engagement. Here's how to identify and define your target audience:

1. **Conduct Market Research**: Start by gathering data about your existing customers and potential audience. Use tools like surveys, interviews, and analytics to understand their demographics, behaviors, preferences, and pain points. Market research provides valuable insights into who your audience is and what they need.

2. **Create Buyer Personas**: Buyer personas are semi-fictional representations of your ideal customers based on real data and insights. They help you visualize and understand your audience's motivations, challenges, and goals. Develop detailed personas that include information such as age, gender, occupation, income, interests, and buying behavior.

3. **Divide Your Audience**: Your audience is made up of different people. Segment your audience into distinct groups based on shared characteristics or behaviors. This allows you to tailor your content to specific segments, making it more relevant and effective. Common segmentation criteria include demographics, psychographics, behavior, and geographic location.

4. **Analyze Competitors**: Look at your competitors to see who they are targeting and how they are engaging their audience. Find weaknesses in their approach that you can exploit. Competitive analysis helps you refine your target audience and find opportunities to differentiate your content.

5. **Continuously Update Your Audience Insights**: Your audience's needs and preferences may change over time. Regularly update your audience research and personas to ensure that your content remains relevant and effective. Use feedback, analytics, and ongoing market research to stay in tune with your audience.

Content Marketing Funnel

A content marketing funnel guides your audience through the buyer's journey, from initial awareness to final conversion. Here's how to develop and optimize a content marketing funnel:

1. **Awareness Stage**: At the top of the funnel, your goal is to attract and engage a broad audience. Create content that addresses common questions, pain points, and interests. This could include blog posts, social media updates, videos, infographics, and educational content. Focus on providing value and building trust.

2. **Consideration Stage**: In the middle of the funnel, your audience is evaluating their options and considering different solutions. Provide more detailed and in-depth content that highlights your expertise and the benefits of your offerings. This could include case studies, whitepapers, ebooks, webinars, and comparison guides. Help your audience make informed decisions.

3. **Conversion Stage**: At the bottom of the funnel, your audience is ready to make a purchase decision. Create content that encourages action and conversion. This could include product demos, free trials, testimonials, pricing information, and detailed product descriptions. Ensure that your calls-to-action are clear and compelling.

4. **Retention Stage**: After the conversion, focus on retaining and nurturing your customers. Provide content that helps them get the most out of your product or service. This could include onboarding guides, how-to videos, user manuals, and customer success stories. Engage with your customers through email newsletters, loyalty programs, and personalized content.

5. **Advocacy Stage**: Encourage satisfied customers to become brand advocates. Create content that makes it easy for them to share their positive experiences. This could include referral programs, user-generated content campaigns, and social media contests. Leverage testimonials, reviews, and case studies to build social proof and attract new customers.

Developing a content marketing strategy involves setting clear goals and objectives, identifying your target audience, and creating a content marketing funnel that guides your audience through the buyer's journey. By following these steps, you can create a strategic and effective content marketing plan that drives engagement, builds trust, and achieves your business goals. As we move into the next chapter, we'll explore content planning and ideation techniques to help you generate and organize content ideas effectively.

CHAPTER 4

CONTENT PLANNING AND IDEATION

Developing a solid content marketing strategy starts with effective planning and ideation. In this chapter, we'll explore techniques for topic research and ideation, how to create a content calendar, and the various types of content formats you can use to engage your audience.

Topic Research and Ideation Techniques

Generating relevant and engaging content ideas is crucial for maintaining a consistent content flow. Here are some techniques to help you with topic research and ideation:

1. **Audience Research**: Begin by learning about the requirements, passions, and problems of your audience. Use surveys, interviews, social media polls, and feedback forms to gather insights. Knowing what your audience cares about will help you create content that resonates with them.

2. **Keyword Research**: Find the terms and phrases that people are using to find you. Use tools like Google Keyword Planner, Ahrefs, and SEMrush to find popular and relevant keywords. This will not only help you generate content ideas but also improve your SEO.

3. **Competitor Analysis**: Look at what your competitors are doing. Analyze their content to see what topics are performing well and where there might be gaps you can fill. Tools like BuzzSumo can help you identify top-performing content in your industry.

4. **Industry Trends and News**: Stay updated with the latest trends and news in your industry. Follow relevant blogs, news sites, and social media channels. Trending topics can provide timely and relevant content ideas.

5. **Content Performance Analysis**: Review your existing content to see what has performed well in the past. Analyzing metrics such as page views, engagement, and social shares can help you understand what topics resonate with your audience and inspire future content.

6. **Brainstorming Sessions**: Regularly conduct brainstorming sessions with your team. Use techniques like mind mapping, where you start with a central idea

and branch out into related topics. Promote teamwork and creativity to provide a variety of ideas.

7. **Customer Feedback and Questions**: Pay attention to the questions and feedback you receive from customers. This can be a goldmine for content ideas, as it directly addresses your audience's needs and concerns.

8. **Content Gaps Analysis**: Identify gaps in your content by analyzing what topics you haven't covered yet but are relevant to your audience. Use tools like Ahrefs' Content Gap tool to find keyword gaps between your site and your competitors'.

Creating a Content Calendar

A content calendar is an essential tool for organizing and scheduling your content. It helps you plan your content strategy, maintain consistency, and ensure timely delivery. This is how to make a content calendar that works:

1. **Define Your Goals and Objectives**: Start by revisiting your content marketing goals and objectives. Your content calendar should align with these goals and help you achieve them. For example, if your goal is to

increase brand awareness, schedule content that boosts visibility and engagement.

2. **Determine Your Content Themes and Topics**: Based on your topic research and ideation, outline the main themes and topics you want to cover. This helps ensure a balanced mix of content that addresses different aspects of your audience's needs.

3. **Choose Your Content Formats**: Decide on the types of content formats you will use (e.g., blog posts, videos, infographics). Diversifying your content formats can help keep your audience engaged and cater to different preferences.

4. **Set a Publishing Schedule**: Determine how often you will publish content. This could be daily, weekly, or monthly, depending on your resources and goals. Select a routine you can stick to since consistency is essential.

5. **Assign Responsibilities**: Clearly define who is responsible for creating, editing, and publishing each piece of content. This ensures accountability and helps streamline the content creation process.

6. **Use a Content Calendar Tool**: Use tools like Google Calendar, Trello, Asana, or dedicated content calendar software to organize and visualize your schedule. These tools can help you track deadlines, assign tasks, and collaborate with your team.

7. **Include Key Dates and Events**: Mark important dates, holidays, industry events, and product launches on your calendar. This helps you plan timely and relevant content around these events.

8. **Review and Adjust Regularly**: Your content calendar should be a flexible tool that evolves with your needs. Regularly review and adjust it based on content performance, audience feedback, and changing priorities.

Types of Content Formats

Diversifying your content formats is essential for engaging different segments of your audience. The following are some common content types and their advantages:

1. **Blog Posts**: Blog posts are a versatile and widely-used content format. They allow you to explore topics in-depth, provide valuable information, and improve your SEO. Blog posts can range from how-to guides and listicles to opinion pieces and industry news.

2. **Videos**: Videos are highly engaging and can convey information quickly and effectively. They are ideal for product demonstrations, tutorials, interviews, and storytelling. Platforms like YouTube and social media make it easy to share video content and reach a broad audience.

3. **Infographics**: Infographics combine visuals and text to present information in a clear and engaging way. They are excellent for simplifying complex data, making statistics more digestible, and providing step-by-step guides. Infographics may generate a lot of traffic and are very shareable.

4. **Ebooks and Whitepapers**: These long-form content formats provide detailed and comprehensive information on specific topics. Ebooks and whitepapers are valuable resources that can be used for lead generation. In order to expand your email list, provide them your contact information in return.

5. **Podcasts**: Podcasts cater to audiences who prefer audio content. They are great for discussing industry topics, interviewing experts, and sharing insights. Listening to podcasts while on the go is handy for those who have busy lives.

6. **Social Media Posts**: Social media platforms are ideal for sharing short, impactful content. Use them to promote your blog posts, videos, infographics, and other content. Social media posts help drive traffic to your website and engage with your audience in real-time.

7. **Case Studies**: Case studies showcase real-life examples of how your products or services have helped customers achieve their goals. They provide social proof and are persuasive in demonstrating your value. Use case studies to highlight success stories and best practices.

8. **Email Newsletters**: Email newsletters allow you to deliver personalized content directly to your audience's inbox. Use them to share updates, promote new content, and keep your audience informed. One of the most effective tools for nurturing leads and preserving client relationships is email marketing.

9. **Webinars and Live Streams**: These interactive formats enable you to engage with your audience in real-time. Use webinars and live streams for live demonstrations, Q&A sessions, and in-depth discussions. They provide a platform for direct interaction and immediate feedback.

Effective content planning and ideation are the cornerstones of a successful content marketing strategy. By conducting thorough topic research, creating a well-organized content calendar, and utilizing diverse content formats, you can ensure that your content resonates with your audience and drives engagement. As we move into the next chapter, we'll explore how to create high-quality content that captivates your audience and achieves your marketing goals.

CHAPTER 5

CREATING HIGH-QUALITY CONTENT

High-quality content is the cornerstone of any successful content marketing strategy. In this chapter, we will delve into the essentials of writing compelling blog posts, crafting engaging videos, and designing effective infographics and visuals. By mastering these content formats, you can capture your audience's attention, provide value, and drive engagement.

Writing Compelling Blog Posts

Blog posts are one of the most versatile and powerful content formats available. Here's how to create blog posts that resonate with your audience:

1. **Understand Your Audience**: Before you start writing, understand who your audience is and what they care about. Use the insights gained from your audience research and buyer personas to tailor your content to their needs, preferences, and pain points.

2. **Choose Relevant and Engaging Topics**: Select topics that are relevant to your audience and aligned with your content marketing goals. Use keyword research to identify popular search terms and address trending topics in your industry. Make sure your topics provide value, whether it's through education, entertainment, or solving a problem.

3. **Craft a Compelling Headline**: Your headline is the first thing readers see, and it determines whether they will click on your post. Make it attention-grabbing, clear, and concise. Use power words, numbers, and questions to pique interest. For example, "10 Proven Strategies to Boost Your SEO Rankings" or "How to Create Engaging Videos That Convert."

4. **Write a Strong Introduction**: The introduction should hook your readers and encourage them to keep reading. Start with a compelling opening sentence that addresses a pain point, poses a question, or shares an interesting fact. Indicate the post's goal and the knowledge that readers should anticipate.

5. **Provide Valuable and Well-Structured Content**: Deliver on the promise made in your headline and introduction. Provide clear, actionable, and valuable information. Use subheadings, bullet points, and numbered lists to break up the text and make it easy to read. Ensure your content flows logically and covers all the necessary points.

6. **Incorporate Visuals and Examples**: Enhance your blog post with relevant images, infographics, charts, and videos. Visuals make your content more engaging and help explain complex concepts. Use real-life examples and case studies to illustrate your points and provide credibility.

7. **Optimize for SEO**: Implement on-page SEO best practices to improve your blog post's visibility in search engines. Use your target keywords naturally throughout the post, including in the title, headings, and meta description. Optimize images with alt text and ensure your content is easy to read with proper formatting.

8. **Include a Call-to-Action (CTA)**: End your blog post with a clear and compelling CTA. Whether you want readers to subscribe to your newsletter, download an ebook, or leave a comment, make sure your CTA is specific and aligned with your goals.

9. **Edit and Proofread**: Before publishing, thoroughly edit and proofread your blog post. Check for grammar, spelling, and punctuation errors. Make sure your writing is jargon-free, succinct, and straightforward. Consider having a colleague review your post for additional feedback.

Crafting Engaging Videos

Video content is incredibly effective for capturing attention and conveying information quickly. Here's how to create videos that engage and convert:

1. **Define Your Purpose and Audience**: Clearly define the purpose of your video and who it's for. Is your goal to inspire, amuse, or educate people? Tailor your video content to meet the needs and preferences of your target audience.

2. **Plan Your Content**: Outline the key points you want to cover and create a storyboard if necessary. Planning helps ensure your video stays focused and delivers a clear message. Consider the length of your video; shorter videos (under 2 minutes) often perform better for keeping viewer attention.

3. **Write a Script**: Write a script to guide your video production. Keep it concise and conversational. Use a natural tone and avoid jargon. Practice delivering your script to ensure it flows smoothly and sounds engaging.

4. **Invest in Quality Production**: While you don't need a professional studio, ensure your video production is of good quality. Use a decent camera, proper lighting,

and clear audio. Poor production quality can distract from your message and diminish viewer engagement.

5. **Engage Your Audience Quickly**: Capture your viewers' attention within the first few seconds. Start with a compelling hook, such as an interesting fact, a question, or a bold statement. Clearly state what the video is about and why it's worth watching.

6. **Use Visuals and Graphics**: Enhance your video with visuals, graphics, and text overlays. These elements can help illustrate your points and make your video more engaging. Use B-roll footage to add variety and keep the visual interest high.

7. **Include a Clear Call-to-Action (CTA)**: Just like with blog posts, include a clear and compelling CTA in your video. Whether you want viewers to subscribe, visit your website, or share the video, make sure your CTA is specific and easy to follow.

8. **Optimize for SEO**: Optimize your video for search engines by using relevant keywords in the title, description, and tags. Create an engaging thumbnail and write a compelling description that includes links to related content. Host your videos on platforms like YouTube to increase discoverability.

9. **Promote Your Video**: Share your video across your marketing channels, including your website, social media, and email newsletters. Encourage your audience to share the video and engage with it through comments and likes.

Designing Infographics and Visuals

Infographics and visuals are powerful tools for simplifying complex information and making your content more shareable. Here's how to design effective infographics and visuals:

1. **Identify Your Key Message**: Determine the main message or data you want to convey with your infographic. Focus on a single topic or set of related data points to avoid overwhelming your audience.

2. **Gather and Organize Data**: Collect accurate and relevant data to support your key message. Organize the data logically, and identify the most important points to highlight. Use reliable sources and provide proper attribution if necessary.

3. **Choose a Simple Layout**: Design your infographic with a clean and simple layout. Use a grid structure to align elements and ensure a balanced composition. Avoid clutter and keep the design focused on delivering your key message clearly.

4. **Use Visual Hierarchy**: Establish a visual hierarchy to guide the viewer's eye through the infographic. Use larger fonts and bold colors for headings and key points. Break up the information into sections with clear subheadings.

5. **Incorporate Visual Elements**: Use charts, graphs, icons, and illustrations to represent your data visually. Choose visuals that enhance understanding and are easy to interpret. Ensure that your visuals are consistent in style and color scheme.

6. **Keep Text Concise**: Use concise and clear text to complement your visuals. Avoid long paragraphs and jargon. Use bullet points and short sentences to make the information easy to digest.

7. **Select a Cohesive Color Scheme**: Choose a color scheme that aligns with your brand and enhances readability. Use contrasting colors to highlight key

points and ensure that the text stands out against the background.

8. **Use Legible Fonts**: Select fonts that are easy to read at various sizes. Use a combination of serif and sans-serif fonts to create contrast and visual interest. Ensure that your text is legible on different devices and screen sizes.

9. **Optimize for Sharing**: Design your infographic with social sharing in mind. Include your logo and website URL for branding. Save the infographic in a high-resolution format and provide options for sharing on social media and embedding on websites.

Creating high-quality content, whether it's blog posts, videos, or infographics, requires careful planning, execution, and optimization. By following these guidelines, you can produce content that captivates your audience, provides value, and drives engagement. As we move into the next chapter, we'll explore the fundamentals of SEO and how it can enhance your content marketing efforts.

PART 2: SEO Essentials

CHAPTER 6

INTRODUCTION TO SEO

One of the most important elements of any digital marketing plan is search engine optimization, or SEO. It ensures that your content is discoverable, drives organic traffic to your website, and enhances your online presence. In this chapter, we'll explore what SEO is and why it matters, how search engines work, and the key SEO terms and concepts you need to understand.

What is SEO and Why It Matters

SEO stands for Search Engine Optimization. It is the practice of optimizing your website and content to rank higher in search engine results pages (SERPs) for relevant keywords and phrases. SEO aims to increase the quantity and quality of organic (non-paid) traffic to your website.

Why SEO Matters:

1. **Visibility and Rankings**: Higher rankings in search results lead to increased visibility for your website. Most users do not scroll past the first page of search results, so achieving a top position is crucial for attracting organic traffic.

2. **Organic Traffic**: SEO drives targeted organic traffic to your website. Unlike paid advertising, organic traffic is cost-effective and sustainable in the long term. Users who find your site through search are often more engaged and likely to convert.

3. **Credibility and Trust**: High search rankings signal to users that your site is authoritative and trustworthy. Search engines like Google prioritize websites that provide a good user experience and high-quality content, enhancing your credibility.

4. **User Experience**: SEO involves optimizing your site's structure, speed, and mobile-friendliness, all of which contribute to a better user experience. A well-optimized site is easy to navigate, loads quickly, and is accessible on all devices.

5. **Competitive Advantage**: Effective SEO can give you a competitive edge. By outranking competitors for key search terms, you can capture a larger share of organic traffic and establish your brand as a leader in your industry.

How Search Engines Work

Understanding how search engines work is fundamental to mastering SEO. To evaluate the authority and relevance of online sites, search engines such as Google employ sophisticated algorithms. Here's a simplified overview of the process:

1. **Crawling**: Search engines use bots, also known as spiders or crawlers, to explore the web. These crawlers find fresh and updated material by following links from one page to another. Crawlers collect information about each page, including its content, structure, and links.

2. **Indexing**: After crawling, search engines index the pages they discover. Storing and classifying the data gathered during crawling is known as indexing. Indexed pages are then added to the search engine's database, making them eligible to appear in search results.

3. **Ranking**: When a user performs a search, the search engine uses its algorithm to rank the indexed pages. The algorithm considers hundreds of factors, including keyword relevance, content quality, user experience, and backlinks. Giving the user the most pertinent and helpful results is the aim.

Key Factors Search Engines Consider:

1. **Relevance**: Search engines assess how closely a page's content matches the user's query. Keywords in the title, headings, and body text play a significant role in determining relevance.

2. **Quality**: High-quality content that provides value to users is prioritized. Factors such as length, originality, accuracy, and comprehensiveness influence content quality.

3. **User Experience**: A positive user experience is crucial. Factors such as page load speed, mobile-friendliness, and ease of navigation impact rankings.

4. **Authority**: Authority is determined by the quality and quantity of backlinks from other reputable websites. Pages with strong backlink profiles are considered more authoritative.

5. **Engagement**: User engagement metrics, such as click-through rates, bounce rates, and time spent on the page, provide insights into how users interact with the content.

Key SEO Terms and Concepts

To effectively implement SEO strategies, it's important to understand key terms and concepts. Here are some essential SEO terms:

1. **Keywords**: Keywords are words and phrases that users type into search engines. They are the foundation of SEO. Understanding which keywords your audience uses helps you create content that meets their needs.

2. **On-Page SEO**: To rank better and attract more relevant traffic, individual web pages are optimized as part of on-page SEO. It includes elements like title tags, meta descriptions, headings, content, and internal links.

3. **Off-Page SEO**: Off-page SEO refers to actions taken outside your website to impact your rankings. The most important aspect is building high-quality backlinks from other reputable sites.

4. **Technical SEO**: Technical SEO focuses on optimizing the technical aspects of your website. This includes improving site speed, ensuring mobile-friendliness, using structured data, and creating an XML sitemap.

5. **Backlinks**: Backlinks, or inbound links, are links from other websites to your site. They are a major ranking factor. High-quality backlinks from reputable websites tell search engines that your material is reliable and useful.

6. **SERP (Search Engine Results Page)**: The SERP is the page displayed by a search engine in response to a user's query. Featured snippets, sponsored advertising, and organic results are all included.

7. **Meta Tags**: Meta tags are snippets of text that describe a page's content. They are present in the page's source code rather than on the actual page. The title tag and meta description are two crucial meta tags.

8. **Alt Text**: Alt text is a description of an image used by search engines to understand what the image is about. Users who are visually challenged can also utilize screen readers to describe visuals.

9. **Anchor content**: An anchor hyperlink's clickable content is called an anchor text. It must be pertinent to the page that is linked. Search engines use anchor text to understand the context of the linked content.

10. **Bounce Rate**: Bounce rate is the percentage of visitors who leave a site after viewing only one page. A high bounce rate might be a sign of irrelevant or uninteresting material.

11. **CTR (Click-Through Rate)**: CTR is the percentage of users who click on a link compared to the total number of users who view the page or SERP. A higher CTR indicates that the link is appealing to users.

12. **Domain Authority (DA)**: DA is a metric developed by Moz that predicts how well a website will rank in search engine results. It's based on factors like age, popularity, and size of the domain.

13. **Page Authority (PA)**: Similar to DA, PA is a metric that predicts how well a specific page will rank. It's influenced by the number and quality of backlinks to the page.

One dynamic and crucial component of digital marketing is SEO. By understanding what SEO is, how search engines work, and the key terms and concepts involved, you can effectively optimize your content to improve visibility, drive organic traffic, and achieve your marketing goals. As we move into the next chapter, we'll dive into the importance of keyword research, the tools available, and the difference between long-tail and short-tail keywords.

CHAPTER 7

KEYWORD RESEARCH

Researching keywords is the cornerstone of every effective SEO plan. It helps you understand what your audience is searching for and how to create content that meets their needs. In this chapter, we'll explore the importance of keyword research, the tools you can use to conduct it, and the difference between long-tail and short-tail keywords.

Importance of Keyword Research

Keyword research is crucial for several reasons:

1. **Understanding Audience Intent**: Keywords reflect the questions, problems, and interests of your audience. By identifying the keywords they use, you can better understand their intent and create content that addresses their needs.

2. **Guiding Content Creation**: Effective keyword research helps you generate ideas for blog posts, articles, videos, and other content formats. It ensures your

content is relevant and aligned with what your audience is looking for.

3. **Improving SEO**: Keywords are the backbone of SEO. By optimizing your content with relevant keywords, you increase the chances of ranking higher in search engine results pages (SERPs). As a result, your website receives more natural traffic and visibility.

4. **Competitive Analysis**: Keyword research allows you to analyze your competitors' strategies. You can identify the keywords they are targeting and discover opportunities to outperform them by creating better or more comprehensive content.

5. **Driving Conversions**: Targeting the right keywords can attract visitors who are more likely to convert into customers. By focusing on keywords with high commercial intent, you can drive targeted traffic that is ready to take action.

Tools for Keyword Research

You may do efficient keyword research with the aid of several tools. These are a few of the most well-liked and practical ones:

1. **Google Keyword Planner**: Provides keyword suggestions, search traffic information, and degrees of competition. This is a free service from Google Ads. It's a great starting point for discovering new keywords and understanding their potential impact.

2. **Ahrefs**: With a strong keyword research capability, Ahrefs is a feature-rich SEO tool. It provides keyword ideas, search volume, keyword difficulty, and click-through rate (CTR) data. Ahrefs also allows you to analyze competitors' keywords and content.

3. **SEMrush**: SEMrush is another popular SEO tool that offers extensive keyword research capabilities. It offers competition analysis, search volume, keyword difficulty, and keyword suggestions. SEMrush also includes features for tracking keyword rankings and optimizing content.

4. **Moz Keyword Explorer**: Moz's keyword research tool offers keyword suggestions, search volume, keyword difficulty, and organic click-through rate data. It also provides a unique metric called "Priority," which helps you identify the most valuable keywords to target.

5. **Ubersuggest**: Ubersuggest is a user-friendly tool that provides keyword ideas, search volume, keyword difficulty, and SEO metrics. It also offers content ideas and competitor analysis features.

6. **Google Trends**: This free tool allows you to explore trending topics and search queries over time. It's useful for identifying seasonal trends and understanding the popularity of specific keywords.

7. **AnswerThePublic**: This tool generates keyword ideas based on common questions and phrases people search for. It's particularly useful for discovering long-tail keywords and understanding the context behind search queries.

Long-Tail vs. Short-Tail Keywords

Keywords can be categorized into two main types: long-tail and short-tail. Understanding the difference between them is essential for effective keyword targeting.

Short-Tail Keywords:

1. **DEFINITION**: Short-tail keywords, also known as head keywords, are short and broad search terms typically consisting of one or two words. Examples include "shoes," "SEO," and "content marketing."

2. **Search Volume**: Short-tail keywords tend to have high search volumes because they are generic and widely used by searchers.

3. **Competition**: Due to their popularity, short-tail keywords often have high competition, making it difficult to rank for them, especially for new or smaller websites.

4. **Intent**: The search intent behind short-tail keywords is usually broad and less specific. Users may be looking for a variety of information, making it harder to determine their exact needs.

Long-Tail Keywords:

1. **DEFINITION**: Long-tail keywords are longer and more specific search terms, typically consisting of three or more words. Examples include "best running shoes for women," "how to improve SEO rankings," and "content marketing strategy for small businesses."

2. **Search Volume**: Long-tail keywords have lower search volumes compared to short-tail keywords. However, they often attract more targeted traffic because they are specific and closely aligned with user intent.

3. **Competition**: Long-tail keywords usually have lower competition, making it easier to rank for them. This is particularly beneficial for new or niche websites looking to establish their presence in the SERPs.

4. **Intent**: The search intent behind long-tail keywords is more precise. Users searching for long-tail keywords are often further along in the buyer's journey and more likely to convert.

Why Focus on Long-Tail Keywords:

1. **Higher Conversion Rates**: Long-tail keywords attract users who are closer to making a purchase decision. They are more likely to convert because their search queries are specific and aligned with their needs.

2. **Lower Competition**: Targeting long-tail keywords allows you to compete more effectively in the SERPs. With lower competition, you have a better chance of ranking higher and attracting organic traffic.

3. **Targeted Traffic**: Long-tail keywords help you reach a more specific audience. By addressing niche topics and user queries, you can attract visitors who are genuinely interested in your content and offerings.

4. **Content Optimization**: Long-tail keywords provide clear direction for creating valuable and relevant content. By focusing on specific queries, you can produce in-depth and comprehensive content that meets user expectations.

Balancing Short-Tail and Long-Tail Keywords:

While long-tail keywords are important, it's also beneficial to include short-tail keywords in your strategy. Short-tail keywords can drive significant traffic and help establish your authority in broader topics. The key is to find a balance between the two, creating a comprehensive keyword strategy that targets both high-volume, competitive terms and low-volume, specific queries.

Keyword research is a fundamental aspect of SEO that guides your content creation and optimization efforts. By understanding the importance of keyword research, utilizing the right tools, and differentiating between long-tail and short-tail keywords, you can develop an effective keyword strategy that drives targeted traffic and improves your search engine rankings. As we move into the next chapter, we'll explore the essential on-page SEO techniques to optimize your titles, meta descriptions, headers, and images.

CHAPTER 8

ON-PAGE SEO

On-page SEO is the practice of optimizing individual web pages to improve their search engine rankings and earn more relevant traffic. It involves various techniques that enhance the content and HTML source code of a page. In this chapter, we'll delve into three critical aspects of on-page SEO: optimizing titles and meta descriptions, effective use of headers and subheaders, and image optimization and alt text.

Optimizing Titles and Meta Descriptions

TITLES

One of the most crucial on-page SEO factors is the title tag. It communicates the purpose of your page to consumers and search engines alike. A well-optimized title can significantly impact your search rankings and click-through rates (CTR).

Best Practices for Title Tags:

1. **Keyword Placement**: Include your primary keyword at the beginning of the title tag. This helps search engines quickly understand the main topic of your page. It is more productive to use "Content Marketing Strategies for Small Businesses" as opposed to "Small Business Strategies for Content Marketing."

2. **Length**: Keep your title tags between 50-60 characters. This ensures they are fully displayed in the SERPs and not truncated. While there is no strict character limit, concise and compelling titles are more effective.

3. **Unique and Descriptive**: Each title tag on your website should be unique and accurately describe the content of the page. It is not advisable to use the same title on several pages since this might confuse consumers and search engines.

4. **Engaging**: Write titles that are compelling and encourage clicks. Use action words and highlight the benefits or unique aspects of your content. For instance, "Top 10 Tips for Successful Content Marketing" has a higher level of engagement compared to "Content Marketing Tips."

META DESCRIPTIONS

The meta description is a brief summary of a web page's content. Although it doesn't directly affect search rankings, a well-crafted meta description can improve your CTR, which indirectly influences your SEO.

Best Practices for Meta Descriptions

1. **Length**: Keep your meta descriptions between 150-160 characters. This ensures they are fully visible in the SERPs and provide enough information to entice users to click.

2. **Incorporate Keywords**: Include your primary and secondary keywords naturally within the meta description. This helps search engines understand the relevance of your content and highlights key terms for users.

3. **Clear and Concise**: Summarize the main point of your page clearly and concisely. Users should be able to understand what your page is about and what value it offers at a glance.

4. **Call to Action**: Encourage users to click on your link by including a call to action (CTA) in your meta description. Words such as "Discover," "Learn more," or "Find out how" have the power to motivate people to act.

5. **Unique**: Like title tags, each meta description should be unique to avoid duplicate content issues and provide a better user experience.

Effective Use of Headers and Subheaders

Headers and subheaders (H1, H2, H3, etc.) structure your content and make it easier for users and search engines to understand. They break up your content into manageable sections and signal the hierarchy of information on your page.

Best Practices for Headers and Subheaders

1. **H1 Tag**: The H1 tag should include your primary keyword and clearly describe the main topic of your page. Each page should have only one H1 tag to maintain a clear content hierarchy. For example, "Ultimate Guide to Content Marketing" is an effective H1 tag.

2. **Hierarchy**: Use headers (H1, H2, H3, etc.) to create a logical structure for your content. The H1 tag is the main title, H2 tags are used for main sections, H3 tags for subsections, and so on. This not only helps with SEO but also improves the readability of your content.

3. **Keywords**: Incorporate relevant keywords into your headers and subheaders naturally. This helps search engines understand the context of your content and improves your chances of ranking for those keywords.

4. **Descriptive**: Make your headers descriptive to give users a clear idea of what each section is about. Avoid vague headers like "Section 1" and use specific phrases like "Benefits of Content Marketing."

5. **Readable**: Use headers to break up long blocks of text and make your content more scannable. Users often skim through content, and clear headers help them find the information they're looking for quickly.

Image Optimization and Alt Text

Images enhance the visual appeal of your content and can improve user engagement. However, they also need to be optimized for SEO to ensure they don't slow down your site and are accessible to search engines.

Best Practices for Image Optimization

1. **File Names**: Use descriptive, keyword-rich file names for your images. Instead of "IMG1234.jpg," use a file name like "content-marketing-strategies.jpg." This helps search engines understand the context of the image.

2. **File Size**: Optimize your images to reduce their file size without compromising quality. Large images can slow down your page load times, negatively impacting

user experience and SEO. Tools like TinyPNG or ImageOptim can help compress images.

3. **File Format**: Choose the appropriate file format for your images. JPEG is typically best for photos, PNG for graphics with transparent backgrounds, and SVG for scalable vector graphics.

4. **Alt Text**: Alt text (alternative text) describes the content of an image for search engines and visually impaired users. Include relevant keywords in your alt text, but avoid keyword stuffing. For example, "A graph showing content marketing trends in 2024" is a good alt text description.

5. **Captions**: Use captions where appropriate. Captions can provide additional context for your images and improve user engagement. They are also read by search engines, so including keywords can be beneficial.

6. **Lazy Loading**: Implement lazy loading for images to improve page load times. Lazy loading defers the loading of images until they are needed, which can significantly enhance the performance of your site.

On-page SEO is a critical aspect of your overall SEO strategy. By optimizing titles and meta descriptions, using headers and subheaders effectively, and optimizing images with proper file names, sizes, formats, and alt text, you can improve your search engine rankings and provide a better user experience. As we move into the next chapter, we'll explore the technical aspects of SEO, including website speed and performance, mobile-friendliness and responsive design, and the importance of XML sitemaps and robots.txt files.

CHAPTER 9

TECHNICAL SEO

Technical SEO focuses on improving the technical aspects of your website to enhance its performance, accessibility, and search engine visibility. It involves optimizing elements like website speed, mobile-friendliness, and the proper use of XML sitemaps and robots.txt files. In this chapter, we'll explore these crucial components of technical SEO in-depth.

Website Speed and Performance

Speed of a website is important for SEO and user experience. A fast-loading website not only provides a better experience for visitors but also ranks higher in search engine results. Slow websites can frustrate users, leading to higher bounce rates and lower engagement.

Best Practices for Improving Website Speed

1. **Optimize Images**: Large image files can significantly slow down your website. Use image compression tools like TinyPNG or ImageOptim to reduce file sizes without compromising quality. Choose the appropriate file format (JPEG, PNG, SVG) for your images.

2. **Enable Browser Caching**: Browser caching stores static files, such as images, CSS, and JavaScript, on a user's device, reducing load times for repeat visitors. Configure your server to enable caching and set appropriate expiration times.

3. **Minify CSS, JavaScript, and HTML**: Minification removes unnecessary characters from your code, such as spaces, commas, and comments, reducing file sizes and improving load times. UglifyJS and CSSNano are two tools that might be useful in this process.

4. **Use a Content Delivery Network (CDN)**: A CDN distributes your website's content across multiple servers worldwide, ensuring faster load times for users

regardless of their location. Cloudflare, Amazon CloudFront, and Akamai are a few well-known CDNs.

5. **Reduce HTTP Requests**: Each element on your webpage (images, scripts, stylesheets) requires an HTTP request. Reduce the number of requests by combining CSS and JavaScript files, using CSS sprites for images, and eliminating unnecessary elements.

6. **Enable Gzip Compression**: Gzip compression reduces the size of your website's files before sending them to the user's browser. Most web servers support Gzip, and it can significantly reduce load times.

7. **Optimize Server Response Time**: A slow server can negatively impact your website's performance. Choose a reliable hosting provider and optimize your server settings to ensure fast response times.

8. **Implement Lazy Loading**: Lazy loading defers the loading of non-essential resources, such as images and videos, until they are needed. This can improve initial page load times and overall performance.

Mobile-Friendliness and Responsive Design

A website must be mobile-friendly given the rise in the popularity of mobile surfing. Google indexes and ranks websites primarily using their mobile form, a practice known as "mobile-first indexing.". A responsive design ensures your website looks and functions well on all devices.

Best Practices for Mobile-Friendliness

1. **Responsive Design**: Use responsive web design to ensure your website adapts to different screen sizes and orientations. CSS media queries and flexible grid layouts can help achieve a responsive design.

2. **Mobile-Friendly Navigation**: Simplify navigation for mobile users by using clear and concise menus, large touch targets, and easy-to-use buttons. Avoid complex dropdowns and multi-level menus.

3. **Optimize for Touch**: Ensure that interactive elements, such as buttons and links, are large enough and spaced adequately to be easily tapped with a finger. This improves usability on touchscreens.

4. **Fast Mobile Load Times**: Mobile users expect fast-loading websites. Optimize images, use efficient coding practices, and leverage caching and CDNs to improve mobile load times.

5. **Avoid Flash and Pop-Ups**: Flash is not supported on most mobile devices, and pop-ups can be intrusive and difficult to close on small screens. Use HTML5 for animations and avoid disruptive pop-ups.

6. **Test on Multiple Devices**: Regularly test your website on various mobile devices and browsers to ensure it performs well across different platforms. Tools like Google's Mobile-Friendly Test can help identify issues.

XML Sitemaps and Robots.txt

XML sitemaps and robots.txt files play crucial roles in how search engines crawl and index your website. Understanding and properly configuring these files can enhance your site's SEO.

XML SITEMAPS

An XML sitemap is a file that helps search engines find and index your material more quickly. It enumerates all the key pages on your website.

Best Practices for XML Sitemaps

1. **Include Important Pages**: Ensure your XML sitemap includes all the important pages of your website that you want to be indexed by search engines. This includes blog posts, product pages, and category pages.

2. **Update Regularly**: Keep your sitemap up to date by automatically generating it whenever new content is added or existing content is updated. Many CMS

platforms, like WordPress, have plugins that handle this for you.

3. **Submit to Search Engines**: Submit your XML sitemap to search engines like Google and Bing through their respective webmaster tools (Google Search Console and Bing Webmaster Tools). This helps search engines discover your content more quickly.

4. **Use Multiple Sitemaps if Necessary**: If your website has a large number of pages, consider using multiple sitemaps and a sitemap index file to manage them. This can help keep your sitemaps within the recommended size limits.

ROBOTS.TXT

The robots.txt file is a simple text file that instructs search engine crawlers on which pages or sections of your website should not be crawled or indexed.

Best Practices for Robots.txt

1. **Block Unimportant Pages**: Use the robots.txt file to block crawlers from accessing pages that are not important for SEO, such as admin pages, login pages, or duplicate content.

2. **Allow Important Pages**: Ensure that important pages you want to be indexed are not blocked by the robots.txt file. Accidentally blocking key pages can negatively impact your search rankings.

3. **Specify Sitemap Location**: Include the location of your XML sitemap in the robots.txt file to help search engines find it. For example: `Sitemap: https://www.yoursite.com/sitemap.xml`

4. **Test Your Robots.txt File**: Use tools like Google Search Console's robots.txt Tester to ensure your file is correctly configured and not blocking important content.

5. **Avoid Overuse**: Use the robots.txt file judiciously. Overuse of disallow directives can prevent search engines from crawling and indexing important content on your site.

Technical SEO is a fundamental aspect of your overall SEO strategy. By focusing on website speed and performance, ensuring mobile-friendliness and responsive design, and properly configuring XML sitemaps and robots.txt files, you can enhance your site's search engine visibility and user experience. As we move into the next chapter, we'll explore content optimization techniques for SEO, including writing SEO-friendly content, incorporating keywords naturally, and optimizing content length and readability.

PART 3: INTEGRATING CONTENT MARKETING AND SEO

CHAPTER 10

CONTENT OPTIMIZATION FOR SEO

Optimizing content for SEO is essential for ensuring that your web pages rank highly in search engine results, attract the right audience, and drive meaningful engagement. In this chapter, we will discuss three critical aspects of content optimization: writing SEO-friendly content, incorporating keywords naturally, and ensuring content length and readability.

Writing SEO-Friendly Content

Creating SEO-friendly content is about striking a balance between making your content appealing to both search engines and human readers. It involves using keywords strategically, providing valuable information, and ensuring your content is well-structured.

Best Practices for Writing SEO-Friendly Content

1. **Understand User Intent**: Before you start writing, understand what your audience is looking for. Are they seeking information, looking to make a purchase, or just browsing? Tailor your content to meet these needs by addressing common questions and providing comprehensive answers.

2. **Keyword Research**: Find out which terms your target audience is using by conducting in-depth keyword research. Use tools like Google Keyword Planner, Ahrefs, or SEMrush to find relevant keywords and understand their search volume and competition.

3. **Engaging Titles and Headlines**: Craft compelling titles and headlines that include your primary keywords and entice users to click. A good headline is clear, concise, and promises value. For example, "10 Proven Strategies for Effective Content Marketing" is more engaging than "Content Marketing Tips."

4. **Provide Value**: Ensure your content is informative, actionable, and valuable to your readers. Answer questions, solve problems, and offer insights that your audience can't find elsewhere. High-quality content is

more likely to be shared and linked to, improving your SEO.

5. **Use Subheadings**: Break your content into sections using subheadings (H2, H3, etc.). This makes your content easier to read and helps search engines understand the structure of your page. When appropriate, incorporate keywords into your subheadings.

6. **Multimedia Elements**: Enhance your content with images, videos, infographics, and other multimedia elements. These can make your content more engaging and provide additional opportunities for optimization (e.g., alt text for images).

7. **Internal Linking**: Link to other relevant pages on your website. This helps search engines crawl your site more effectively and keeps users engaged by providing them with additional useful information.

Incorporating Keywords Naturally

Keywords are crucial for SEO, but they need to be incorporated naturally into your content. Overusing keywords, or "keyword stuffing," can degrade user experience and incur search engine penalties.

Best Practices for Natural Keyword Incorporation

1. **Primary Keywords**: Include your primary keyword in the title, first paragraph, and a few times throughout the content. Aim for a keyword density of around 1-2%, meaning your keyword should appear once or twice per 100 words.

2. **Secondary Keywords and Variants**: Use related keywords and synonyms throughout your content to capture a wider range of search queries. This helps your content appear for more search terms and avoids keyword stuffing.

3. **Contextual Usage**: Incorporate keywords in a way that fits naturally within the context of your sentences. Avoid forcing keywords into places where they don't make sense. For example, instead of "best SEO practices use," write "using the best SEO practices."

4. **LSI Keywords**: Latent Semantic Indexing (LSI) keywords are terms that are semantically related to your main keyword. These aid in the context of your content being understood by search engines. In the event where "content marketing" is your main keyword, some examples of LSI keywords include "digital marketing," "content strategy," and "online marketing."

5. **Anchor Text**: When linking to other pages on your site or external resources, use descriptive anchor text that includes relevant keywords. This helps search engines understand the content of the linked page and improves your SEO.

6. **Avoid Over-Optimization**: While keywords are important, over-optimizing can harm your SEO. Write primarily for your audience and ensure that your content flows naturally. Search engines are sophisticated enough to understand context and relevance.

Content Length and Readability

The length and readability of your content play significant roles in SEO. Long-form content generally performs better in search rankings, but it must also be easy to read and understand.

Best Practices for Content Length and Readability

1. **Optimal Length**: While there is no one-size-fits-all answer for content length, longer content (1,500 words or more) tends to rank better because it provides more comprehensive information. However, focus on quality over quantity. Ensure that every word adds value and avoids unnecessary fluff.

2. **Readability**: Use clear and concise language to ensure your content is easily understood by a broad audience. Tools like Hemingway Editor or Grammarly can help you simplify your writing and improve readability.

3. **Short Paragraphs**: Break your content into short paragraphs (2-3 sentences each). Large blocks of text can be intimidating and difficult to read, especially on mobile devices.

4. **Bullet Points and Lists**: Use bullet points and numbered lists to present information clearly and concisely. Lists are easier to scan and can highlight key points effectively.

5. **Readable Fonts**: Choose readable fonts and ensure sufficient contrast between text and background. This enhances the user experience and makes your content accessible to a wider audience.

6. **Visual Breaks**: Use images, videos, and other visual elements to break up text and make your content more engaging. Visual breaks can keep readers interested and reduce the likelihood of them leaving your page prematurely.

7. **Consistent Style**: Maintain a consistent writing style and tone throughout your content. This helps build a connection with your audience and makes your content more enjoyable to read.

Optimizing content for SEO involves more than just inserting keywords. It requires a strategic approach to writing, incorporating keywords naturally, and ensuring content length and readability. By following these best practices, you can create content that ranks well in search engine results, attracts the right audience, and keeps readers engaged. In the next chapter, we'll explore link building and the importance of backlinks, including strategies for acquiring quality backlinks and leveraging guest blogging and influencer outreach.

CHAPTER 11

LINK BUILDING AND BACKLINKS

Backlinks are a fundamental component of SEO, acting as votes of confidence from other websites. They signal to search engines that your content is valuable and trustworthy, which can significantly boost your site's search rankings. In this chapter, we'll explore the importance of backlinks, strategies for acquiring quality backlinks, and the roles of guest blogging and influencer outreach in building a robust backlink profile.

Importance of Backlinks

Links from one website to another are called backlinks, sometimes referred to as inbound or incoming links. They are crucial for SEO because search engines like Google view them as endorsements of the linked content's quality and relevance.

Key Reasons Why Backlinks Are Important

1. **Improved Search Engine Rankings**: Backlinks are one of the primary factors that search engines use to rank websites. Pages with a high number of quality backlinks tend to rank higher in search results because they are seen as more authoritative and relevant.

2. **Increased Organic Traffic**: Organic traffic rises as a result of higher search engine ranks. As your pages appear higher in search results, more users are likely to visit your site, leading to greater exposure and potential conversions.

3. **Faster Indexing**: Search engines use bots to crawl the web and index new content. Backlinks help these bots discover your pages faster, ensuring that your new content is indexed more quickly and starts ranking sooner.

4. **Referral Traffic**: Backlinks from high-traffic websites can drive significant referral traffic to your site. Users who click on these links are often interested in your content, which can lead to higher engagement and conversion rates.

5. **Building Authority and Credibility**: Quality backlinks from reputable websites enhance your site's authority and credibility. This not only improves your SEO but also builds trust with your audience, making them more likely to engage with your content and brand.

Strategies for Acquiring Quality Backlinks

Acquiring high-quality backlinks requires a strategic approach. The caliber and applicability of the connecting sites are equally as important as the sheer number of backlinks.

Effective Strategies for Acquiring Quality Backlinks

1. **Create High-Quality Content**: The foundation of any successful link-building strategy is creating high-quality, valuable content that others want to link to. Focus on producing in-depth articles, research studies, infographics, and other types of content that provide unique insights and value.

2. **Conduct Outreach**: Reach out to websites and bloggers in your niche and inform them about your content. Personalize your outreach emails, explaining why your content is relevant to their audience and how it can add value. Building relationships with influencers and industry leaders can also lead to natural backlink opportunities.

3. **Leverage Broken Link Building**: Find broken links on other websites and suggest your content as a replacement. Use tools like Ahrefs or Check My Links to identify broken links on relevant sites. This strategy helps website owners fix broken links while providing you with valuable backlinks.

4. **Use Skyscraper Technique**: Identify top-performing content in your niche and create something even better. Once you've published your superior content, reach out to sites linking to the original piece and suggest they link to your improved version instead.

5. **Participate in Forums and Communities**: Engage in forums, discussion boards, and online communities related to your industry. When appropriate, share your knowledge and include a link to your work.

Be careful not to spam; focus on providing genuine value to the community.

6. **Submit to Directories and Resource Pages**: Submit your website to reputable directories and resource pages that are relevant to your industry. While not as powerful as other strategies, this can still provide valuable backlinks and drive targeted traffic.

7. **Create Shareable Infographics and Visuals**: Infographics and other visual content are highly shareable and can attract backlinks from various websites. Ensure your infographics are well-designed, informative, and easy to understand. Promote them through social media and outreach to relevant websites.

Guest Blogging and Influencer Outreach

Guest blogging and influencer outreach are powerful strategies for acquiring high-quality backlinks and increasing your online presence.

GUEST BLOGGING

Writing content for other websites in your area is known as guest blogging.. It allows you to reach a wider audience, build relationships with other bloggers, and earn valuable backlinks to your site.

Best Practices for Guest Blogging

1. **Identify Target Blogs**: Look for respectable blogs that welcome guest pieces within your sector. Seek out websites with relevant content, active readership, and high domain authority.

2. **Pitch Relevant Topics**: When pitching guest post ideas, propose topics that are relevant to the blog's audience and align with your expertise. Personalize your pitch and explain how your article will provide value to their readers.

3. **Write High-Quality Content**: Ensure your guest post is well-researched, well-written, and provides actionable insights. Include links to your content where relevant, but focus on adding value rather than self-promotion.

4. **Follow standards**: Comply with the host blog's guest blogging standards. This includes word count, formatting, and any specific requirements they may have.

5. **Promote Your Guest Posts**: Once your guest post is published, promote it through your social media channels, email newsletters, and other marketing efforts. This drives traffic to the host blog and demonstrates your commitment to providing value.

INFLUENCER OUTREACH

Influencer outreach involves building relationships with influential individuals in your industry who can help promote your content and provide valuable backlinks.

Best Practices for Influencer Outreach

1. **Identify Relevant Influencers**: Use tools like BuzzSumo, Followerwonk, or social media platforms to find influencers in your niche. Look for individuals with large followings, high engagement rates, and relevant content.

2. **Build Genuine Relationships**: Engage with influencers by commenting on their posts, sharing their content, and participating in conversations. Building genuine relationships increases the likelihood of them sharing your content and linking to your site.

3. **Personalize Your Outreach**: When reaching out to influencers, personalize your messages and explain why your content is relevant to their audience. Highlight how your content can add value and offer to reciprocate by promoting their content as well.

4. **Offer Value**: Provide value to influencers by offering exclusive content, insights, or collaboration opportunities. This can make them more likely to share your content and provide backlinks.

5. **Track and Follow Up**: Monitor your outreach efforts and follow up with influencers who show interest. Building and maintaining relationships takes time and effort, so be patient and persistent.

Link building is a crucial aspect of any SEO strategy, with backlinks playing a significant role in determining your site's search engine rankings, authority, and traffic. By focusing on acquiring high-quality backlinks through strategies like content creation, outreach, guest blogging, and influencer engagement, you can build a robust backlink profile that enhances your SEO performance. As we move to the next chapter, we'll explore content distribution and promotion techniques, including social media marketing, email marketing campaigns, and paid advertising.

CHAPTER 12

CONTENT DISTRIBUTION AND PROMOTION

Creating high-quality content is only the first step in a successful content marketing strategy. To maximize the reach and impact of your content, you must effectively distribute and promote it. This chapter focuses on three key methods for content distribution and promotion: social media marketing, email marketing campaigns, and paid advertising. Each of these channels plays a vital role in amplifying your content's visibility and driving engagement.

SOCIAL MEDIA MARKETING

Social media platforms offer unparalleled opportunities to distribute content, engage with your audience, and build a community around your brand. Effective social media marketing involves more than just sharing links to your content; it requires strategic planning and engagement.

Key Strategies for Social Media Marketing

1. **Choose the Right Platforms**: Not all social media platforms are created equal. Select platforms that align with your audience and content. For example, LinkedIn is ideal for B2B content, while Instagram and Pinterest are better for visually appealing content.

2. **Create a Content Calendar**: Plan your social media posts in advance using a content calendar. This ensures consistent posting and helps you align your social media activities with your overall content marketing strategy. Include a mix of content types, such as blog posts, videos, infographics, and user-generated content.

3. **Involve Your Audience**: Social media is a mutually beneficial relationship. Interact with your audience by leaving comments, posing queries, and promoting dialogue. Express gratitude for comments and articles contributed by users. This encourages loyalty and creates a sense of community.

4. **Use Hashtags and Keywords**: Hashtags and keywords can increase the visibility of your posts. Look

for trending and pertinent hashtags for your industry, then thoughtfully include them into your postings. Avoid overusing hashtags, as this can make your posts look spammy.

5. **Leverage Visual Content**: Visual content, such as images, videos, and infographics, tends to perform better on social media. Use high-quality visuals to capture attention and enhance your message. Platforms like Instagram and Pinterest are especially effective for visual content.

6. **Analyze Performance**: Use social media analytics tools to track the performance of your posts. Monitor metrics such as likes, shares, comments, and click-through rates to understand what resonates with your audience. Make adjustments to your social media approach using this information.

7. **Collaborate with Influencers**: Partner with influencers in your industry to expand your reach. Influencers can help you tap into their established audience and lend credibility to your content. Make sure the partnerships you enter into are genuine and consistent with your brand.

EMAIL MARKETING CAMPAIGNS

Email marketing remains one of the most effective channels for distributing content and nurturing relationships with your audience. It lets you send individualized content straight to the inboxes of your subscribers.

Key Strategies for Email Marketing Campaigns

1. **Build a Quality Email List**: Focus on building a list of engaged and interested subscribers. Use lead magnets, such as eBooks, webinars, or exclusive content, to encourage sign-ups. Refrain from buying email lists since this might harm your sender reputation and result in low interaction.

2. **Segment Your Audience**: Segment your email list based on demographics, behavior, and preferences. This raises the possibility of interaction by enabling you to provide pertinent and targeted material to various groups.

3. **Craft Compelling Subject Lines**: The subject line is the first thing your subscribers see. Craft compelling and intriguing subject lines that encourage opens. Avoid clickbait tactics, as they can harm your credibility.

4. **Personalize Your Emails**: Personalization goes beyond addressing your subscribers by name. Use data to tailor content based on their interests and behavior. Personalized emails can significantly increase open and click-through rates.

5. **Provide Valuable Content**: Ensure that your emails provide value to your subscribers. Share high-quality content, such as blog posts, case studies, industry insights, and exclusive offers. Pay close attention to problem-solving techniques and audience demands.

6. **Include Clear Calls to Action (CTAs)**: Every email should have a clear and compelling CTA. Whether it's encouraging readers to read a blog post, download a resource, or register for a webinar, make sure your CTA stands out and is easy to follow.

7. **Analyze and Optimize**: Use email marketing analytics to track key metrics, such as open rates,

click-through rates, and conversion rates. Examine this data to determine what functions well and what doesn't. Use this information to continuously enhance your email marketing.

PAID ADVERTISING

Paid advertising can accelerate your content distribution efforts by targeting specific audiences and driving immediate traffic. While it requires an investment, paid advertising can yield significant returns when done strategically.

Key Strategies for Paid Advertising

1. **Choose the Right Platforms**: Select advertising platforms that align with your audience and goals. Google Ads, Facebook Ads, LinkedIn Ads, and Instagram Ads are popular options, each with its unique strengths and targeting capabilities.

2. **Define Your Objectives**: Clearly define your advertising objectives, whether it's increasing website traffic, generating leads, or boosting brand awareness. Your advertising approach and success metrics will be guided by your objectives.

3. **Target Your Audience**: Use detailed targeting options to reach your ideal audience. Take into account variables like demographics, hobbies, habits, and geography. Your adverts will work better if you target them more precisely.

4. **Create Compelling Ad Copy and Visuals**: Craft engaging ad copy and use high-quality visuals to capture attention. Highlight the benefits of your content and include a strong CTA. A/B test several ad versions to see which ones your audience responds to the best.

5. **Set a Budget and Bidding Strategy**: Establish a budget for advertising and select a bidding strategy that fits your objectives. Whether you opt for cost-per-click (CPC), cost-per-impression (CPM), or cost-per-action (CPA), monitor your spending and adjust as needed.

6. **Monitor and Optimize Performance**: Regularly monitor the performance of your ads using analytics tools provided by the advertising platforms. Monitor performance indicators like ROI (return on investment) and click-through/conversion rates. Utilize this information to enhance campaign performance and outcomes.

7. **Retargeting**: Implement retargeting campaigns to re-engage users who have previously interacted with your content or visited your website. Retargeting can help you stay top-of-mind and encourage users to return and convert.

Effective content distribution and promotion require a multi-channel approach that leverages the strengths of social media marketing, email marketing campaigns, and paid advertising. By strategically using these channels, you can maximize the reach and impact of your content, drive engagement, and achieve your marketing goals. In the next chapter, we will delve into advanced SEO techniques, including schema markup and structured data, local SEO strategies, and voice search optimization.

PART 4: ADVANCED STRATEGIES AND TOOLS

CHAPTER 13

ADVANCED SEO TECHNIQUES

As search engine optimization (SEO) continues to evolve, mastering advanced techniques becomes crucial for maintaining and improving your website's visibility and rankings. This chapter explores three advanced SEO techniques: schema markup and structured data, local SEO strategies, and voice search optimization.

SCHEMA MARKUP AND STRUCTURED DATA

One type of microdata you may add to your web pages to improve search engine understanding of your site's content and context is schema markup. It enhances the appearance of your search engine results by providing rich snippets, which can lead to higher click-through rates and improved visibility.

Key Aspects of Schema Markup and Structured Data

1. WHAT IS SCHEMA MARKUP ?

Schema markup is a vocabulary of tags (or microdata) that you add to your HTML to improve the way search engines read and represent your page in search results. It helps search engines understand the meaning of your content beyond just the words on the page.

2. Benefits of Schema Markup

1. **Enhanced Search Results**: Schema markup can lead to rich snippets in search results, such as star ratings, product prices, event dates, and more, making your listings more attractive and informative.

2 **Improved Click-Through Rates**: Rich snippets make your listings stand out, potentially increasing click-through rates (CTR) by providing users with more relevant information upfront.

3. **Better SEO Performance**: While schema markup itself isn't a direct ranking factor, it indirectly impacts SEO by improving user experience and engagement metrics, which can influence rankings.

3. Types of Schema Markup

There are various types of schema markup that you can use depending on your content type, including:

1. **Product**: For e-commerce product details like price, availability, and reviews.

2. **Article**: For news articles, blog posts, and other editorial content.

3. **Event**: For events with details such as date, time, and location.

4. **Organization**: For information about your business or organization.

5. **Local Business**: For local businesses with address, phone number, and opening hours.

6. **FAQ**: For frequently asked questions and their answers.

4. Implementing Schema Markup

You can implement schema markup using JSON-LD (recommended by Google), Microdata, or RDFa formats. Tools like Google's Structured Data Markup Helper can assist you in generating and implementing schema markup for your pages.

LOCAL SEO STRATEGIES

Local SEO focuses on optimizing your website to appear in local search results, particularly when users search for businesses or services near their location. It's essential for companies that have physical sites or that target particular regions.

Effective Local SEO Strategies

1. **Google My Business (GMB)**:

1. Verify and enhance your listing on Google My Business. Ensure your business name, address, and phone number (NAP) are accurate and consistent across all platforms.

2. Add detailed business information, such as business hours, services offered, photos, and customer reviews.

3. Encourage customers to leave reviews on your GMB profile, as positive reviews can improve your local rankings.

2. **Local Keywords and Content**:

1. Use local keywords (e.g., "best pizza New York City") throughout your website's content, meta descriptions, and headings.

2. Create location-specific landing pages or content targeting local events, news, or community initiatives.

3. Include local business schema markup to help search engines understand your business's geographic relevance.

3. **Local Citations and Directory Listings**

1. Ensure your business is listed accurately on local directories, review sites, and industry-specific platforms (e.g., Yelp, TripAdvisor, Yellow Pages).

2. Consistent NAP information across these directories signals credibility to search engines and improves local SEO.

4. **Mobile Optimization**

1. Optimize your website for mobile devices, as many local searches are conducted on smartphones.

2. Ensure your website loads quickly and provides a seamless user experience on mobile devices.

5. Local Link Building

1. Build links from local websites, community organizations, and local news outlets. Local backlinks can signal relevance and authority to search engines for local searches.

VOICE SEARCH OPTIMIZATION

With the rise of voice-enabled devices and virtual assistants like Siri, Alexa, and Google Assistant, optimizing for voice search has become increasingly important. Voice search optimization focuses on understanding and catering to the conversational queries users make via voice commands.

Strategies for Voice Search Optimization

1. Long-Tail Keywords and Natural Language

1. Voice searches tend to be more conversational and longer than text-based searches. Optimize your content for long-tail keywords and natural language queries.

2. Use tools like Answer the Public or SEMrush's Keyword Magic Tool to identify common voice search queries related to your industry.

2. Featured Snippets and Position Zero

1. Aim to appear in featured snippets, also known as position zero, which often provide answers to voice search queries.

2. Structure your content to directly answer common questions your audience might ask. Use headings and bullet points for clarity.

3. Local Voice Search Optimization

1. Apply local SEO strategies to voice search by optimizing for local queries (e.g., "near me" searches).

2. Include local business information in your content and schema markup to improve visibility for local voice searches.

4. Website Speed and Mobile-Friendliness

1. Ensure your website loads quickly on both desktop and mobile devices. Voice search users expect fast and responsive websites.

2. Optimize images, minimize JavaScript, and leverage browser caching to improve loading times.

5. Structured Data and Contextual Relevance

1. Implement structured data markup to provide context and enhance search engines' understanding of your content.

2. Create content that addresses specific user intents and provides comprehensive answers to queries.

Mastering advanced SEO techniques like schema markup and structured data, local SEO strategies, and voice search optimization can significantly enhance your website's visibility and performance in search engine results. These techniques go beyond basic SEO practices to cater to evolving search trends and user behaviors. In the next chapter, we will explore content marketing automation, including tools for automating content distribution, workflow automation, and the benefits and challenges of automation in content marketing.

CHAPTER 14

CONTENT MARKETING AUTOMATION

Automating content marketing processes can streamline your workflow, increase efficiency, and scale your efforts. This chapter explores three key aspects of content marketing automation: tools for automating content marketing, workflow automation, and the benefits and challenges associated with automation.

Tools for Automating Content Marketing

Content marketing automation tools help marketers manage and execute various tasks, from content creation to distribution and analysis. These tools are designed to simplify repetitive tasks, enhance productivity, and improve campaign effectiveness.

Popular Tools for Automating Content Marketing

1. Content Management Systems (CMS):

Platforms like WordPress, Drupal, and Joomla facilitate content creation, publishing, and management. They offer plugins and integrations for scheduling posts, optimizing content for SEO, and managing multimedia.

2. Email Marketing Automation:

Tools such as Mailchimp, HubSpot, and ConvertKit automate email campaigns, segmentation, and personalized messaging. They allow scheduling, A/B testing, and tracking of email performance metrics.

3. Social Media Management:

Tools like Buffer, Hootsuite, and Sprout Social enable scheduling, monitoring, and analytics for multiple social media platforms. They streamline content posting, engagement tracking, and audience management.

4. **Content Curation and RSS Feeds**:

Platforms such as Feedly, Pocket, and Flipboard aggregate content from various sources based on chosen topics or keywords. They automate content discovery, curation, and sharing across channels.

5. **Workflow Automation**:

Tools like Zapier, IFTTT, and Workato automate repetitive tasks and workflows across different apps and platforms. They integrate with CRM systems, email marketing tools, and project management software to streamline processes.

6. **SEO and Analytics**:

Tools such as SEMrush, Moz, and Google Analytics automate keyword tracking, SEO audits, and performance reporting. They provide insights into website traffic, search rankings, and content engagement metrics.

WORKFLOW AUTOMATION

Workflow automation involves using software and tools to streamline and optimize content marketing processes, reducing manual intervention and ensuring consistency in execution.

Benefits of Workflow Automation

1. **Efficiency and Productivity**:

1. Automating repetitive tasks frees up time for marketers to focus on strategy, creativity, and higher-value activities.

2. Standardized workflows ensure consistency in content creation, publishing schedules, and campaign management.

2. **Improved Collaboration**:

1. Automation tools facilitate seamless collaboration among team members, regardless of their location or time zone.

2. Workflow automation assigns tasks, tracks progress, and centralizes communication, reducing delays and miscommunication.

3. **Scalability**:

1. Automated workflows can scale with business growth, accommodating increased content production, audience engagement, and campaign complexity.

2. Templates and predefined rules streamline onboarding for new team members and ensure adherence to best practices.

Benefits and Challenges of Automation

While content marketing automation offers numerous advantages, it also presents challenges that marketers must address to maximize its effectiveness.

BENEFITS

1. **Time Savings**: Automation reduces manual effort, allowing marketers to focus on strategy and creative tasks.

2. **Consistency**: Automated workflows ensure consistent execution of tasks and campaigns.

3. **Data-Driven Decisions**: Automation tools provide actionable insights from data, enabling marketers to optimize campaigns based on performance metrics.

CHALLENGES

1. **Initial Setup Complexity**: Implementing automation tools and workflows requires time and technical expertise.

2. **Risk of Over-Automation**: Over-reliance on automation can lead to impersonal communication and reduced engagement.

3. **Integration Issues**: Ensuring seamless integration between different tools and platforms can be challenging.

Content marketing automation empowers marketers to streamline processes, enhance efficiency, and achieve better campaign outcomes. By leveraging automation tools effectively and addressing potential challenges, organizations can optimize their content marketing efforts and drive business growth. In the next chapter, we will explore analytics and performance measurement in content marketing, including key metrics to track, tools for monitoring performance, and using data-driven insights to refine your strategy.

CHAPTER 15

ANALYTICS AND PERFORMANCE MEASUREMENT

Analyzing and measuring the performance of your content marketing and SEO efforts is crucial for understanding what works, identifying areas for improvement, and maximizing your return on investment (ROI). This chapter explores three essential aspects of analytics and performance measurement: key metrics to track, tools for monitoring and analyzing performance, and using data to refine your strategy.

Key Metrics to Track

Tracking the right metrics helps you assess the effectiveness of your content marketing and SEO strategies, providing actionable insights to optimize performance and achieve your goals.

Key Metrics to Track

1. Traffic Metrics:

1. **Website Traffic**: Monitor total visits, unique visitors, and page views to understand overall website traffic trends.

2. **Organic Search Traffic**: Track the volume of traffic coming from search engines to measure SEO effectiveness.

3. **Referral Traffic**: Analyze traffic from external sources, such as social media platforms, websites, and email campaigns.

2. Engagement Metrics:

1. **Bounce Rate**: Measure the percentage of visitors who leave your site after viewing only one page. A high bounce rate might be a sign of an ineffective user interface or useless information.

2. **Average Session Duration**: Assess how long visitors spend on your site per session, indicating content engagement and user interest.

3. **Pages per Session**: Evaluate the average number of pages viewed per visit, indicating site navigation and content consumption.

3. **Conversion Metrics**:

1. **Conversion Rate**: Calculate the percentage of visitors who complete a desired action, such as filling out a form, making a purchase, or subscribing to a newsletter.

2. **Goal Completions**: Track specific goals configured in Google Analytics, such as form submissions, downloads, or sign-ups.

3. **ROI**: Measure the return on investment from your content marketing efforts, comparing costs (time, resources) with generated revenue or business outcomes.

4. **SEO Performance Metrics**:

1. **Keyword Rankings**: Monitor the ranking positions of targeted keywords in search engine results pages (SERPs).

2. **Backlink Metrics**: Track the quantity and quality of backlinks pointing to your site, assessing their impact on SEO performance.

3. **Domain Authority and Page Authority**: Evaluate the authority and credibility of your website and individual pages.

Tools for Monitoring and Analyzing Performance

Utilizing the right tools is essential for accurate data collection, analysis, and reporting to measure the success of your content marketing and SEO campaigns.

Tools for Monitoring and Analyzing Performance

1. **Google Analytics**:

offers thorough insights into user behavior, website traffic, and conversion data. Track key performance indicators (KPIs) and set up custom reports and goals.

2. **SEO Tools:**

1. **SEMrush**: Offers keyword research, backlink analysis, and site audit tools to optimize SEO strategies.

2. **Moz**: Provides SEO analytics, rank tracking, and link building insights.

3. **Ahrefs**: Offers competitive analysis, keyword research, and content auditing tools.

3. Content Management Systems (CMS):

Platforms like WordPress, HubSpot, and Drupal include built-in analytics dashboards and plugins for tracking content performance, user engagement, and SEO.

4. Social Media Analytics Tools:

1. **Buffer**: Tracks social media engagement, click-through rates, and audience demographics.

2. **Sprout Social**: Provides analytics for social media performance, including follower growth, engagement metrics, and campaign effectiveness.

5. Email Marketing Platforms:

1. **Mailchimp**: Measures email open rates, click-through rates, and conversion rates for email campaigns.

2. **HubSpot**: Offers email marketing analytics, lead nurturing insights, and campaign performance tracking.

Using Data to Refine Your Strategy

Data-driven decision-making empowers marketers to optimize their content marketing and SEO strategies based on actionable insights and performance metrics.

Steps to Refine Your Strategy Using Data

1. **Identify Trends and Patterns**: Analyze data trends to understand what content resonates with your audience, which channels drive the most traffic, and when engagement peaks.

2. **Optimize Content Performance**: Use insights to refine content strategies, focusing on topics, formats, and distribution channels that yield the highest ROI and engagement rates.

3. **Adjust SEO Tactics**: Monitor keyword performance and SEO metrics to identify opportunities

for optimization, such as updating content, improving on-page SEO, or acquiring high-quality backlinks.

4. **Personalize User Experiences**: Use data to segment audiences and deliver personalized content experiences based on user preferences, behaviors, and demographics.

5. **Set Clear Goals and KPIs**: Align data analysis with strategic goals and KPIs to measure success effectively and adjust tactics accordingly.

By leveraging analytics and performance measurement effectively, marketers can continuously improve their content marketing and SEO strategies, drive sustainable growth, and achieve measurable business outcomes.

Understanding and applying analytics and performance measurement techniques is essential for optimizing your content marketing and SEO efforts. In the next chapter, we will explore successful case studies in content marketing and SEO, showcasing examples of effective campaigns, lessons learned from top brands, and strategies to replicate their success.

PART 5: CASE STUDIES AND REAL-WORLD APPLICATIONS

CHAPTER 16

SUCCESSFUL CONTENT MARKETING AND SEO CASE STUDIES

Examining successful case studies in content marketing and SEO provides valuable insights into effective strategies, lessons learned from top brands, and practical steps to replicate their success. Let's explore these aspects in depth.

Examples of Successful Campaigns

Successful content marketing and SEO campaigns demonstrate innovative strategies, exceptional execution, and measurable results. Here are a few notable examples:

1. **Red Bull Stratos:**

1. **Campaign Overview**: Red Bull's Stratos mission involved Felix Baumgartner's record-breaking skydive from the stratosphere. The event was live-streamed, generating immense global attention and media coverage.

2. **Key Success Factors**: Innovative content format (live-streaming), captivating storytelling, and leveraging social media for real-time engagement.

3. **Results**: Increased brand visibility, millions of views across platforms, and strengthened brand association with extreme sports and adventure.

2. **Dove's Real Beauty Campaign:**

1. **Campaign Overview**: Dove's Real Beauty campaign aimed to challenge beauty stereotypes and empower women. It featured real women instead of traditional models, promoting self-confidence and body positivity.

2. **Key Success Factors**: Authentic storytelling, emotional appeal, and creating a movement around a social cause.

3. **Results**: Viral content, increased brand loyalty, and positive brand perception globally.

3. **HubSpot's Inbound Marketing Strategy:**

1. **Campaign Overview**: HubSpot pioneered the inbound marketing methodology, focusing on creating valuable content to attract and engage prospects.

2. **Key Success Factors**: Comprehensive content strategy, SEO optimization, and leveraging content to nurture leads through the sales funnel.

3. **Results**: Significant growth in organic traffic, lead generation, and establishment as a thought leader in digital marketing.

LESSONS LEARNED FROM TOP BRANDS

Top brands that excel in content marketing and SEO offer valuable lessons for marketers looking to achieve similar success:

1. **Focus on Audience Needs**: Successful brands prioritize understanding their audience's pain points, interests, and behaviors to create relevant and valuable content.

2. **Consistency and Long-Term Commitment**: Building a strong brand presence through content marketing and SEO requires consistent effort, long-term strategy, and adapting to evolving trends.

3. **Integration of Channels**: Effective campaigns often integrate multiple channels (e.g., social media, email marketing, SEO) to amplify reach and engagement across platforms.

4. **Data-Driven Decision Making**: Leveraging analytics and performance metrics to refine strategies and optimize content based on what resonates with the audience.

How To Replicate Their Success

Replicating the success of top brands in content marketing and SEO involves strategic planning, creativity, and continuous optimization:

1. **Research and Analysis**: Conduct thorough research on successful campaigns within your industry. Analyze their strategies, audience engagement tactics, and key performance metrics.

2. **Define Clear Objectives**: Set specific goals and KPIs aligned with your business objectives. Determine what success looks like for your content marketing and SEO efforts.

3. **Content Quality and Relevance**: Prioritize creating high-quality content that addresses audience needs, solves problems, or entertains. Ensure content is optimized for SEO to improve discoverability.

4. **Multichannel Distribution**: Utilize a multichannel distribution strategy to reach your target audience across various platforms and touchpoints.

5. **Continuous Learning and Adaptation**: Stay updated with industry trends, algorithm changes, and best practices in content marketing and SEO. Adapt your strategies based on data-driven insights and feedback.

By studying successful case studies, learning from top brands' experiences, and implementing proven strategies, marketers can enhance their content marketing and SEO initiatives to achieve sustainable growth and meaningful results.

Studying successful content marketing and SEO case studies provides valuable insights and inspiration for optimizing your own strategies. In the next chapter, we will explore challenges and solutions in content marketing and SEO, addressing common hurdles faced by marketers, practical solutions, and emerging trends shaping the future of digital marketing.

CHAPTER 17

ISSUES AND REMEDIES IN SEO AND CONTENT MARKETING

Content marketing and SEO are powerful tools for driving traffic, engagement, and conversions, but they come with their own set of challenges. This chapter explores common hurdles marketers face, practical solutions and best practices to overcome them, and future trends to stay ahead in the ever-evolving digital landscape.

COMMON CHALLENGES FACED BY MARKETERS

1. Creating High-Quality Content Consistently:

1. **Challenge**: Producing engaging, valuable content on a regular basis can be resource-intensive and time-consuming.

2. **Impact**: Inconsistent content quality or frequency can lead to decreased audience engagement and lower search rankings.

2. Keeping Up with SEO Algorithm Changes:

1. **Challenge**: Search engine algorithms are constantly evolving, requiring continuous adaptation and updates to SEO strategies.

2. **Impact**: Failing to keep up with changes can result in reduced visibility, traffic, and rankings.

3. Measuring ROI:

1. **Challenge**: Demonstrating the return on investment for content marketing and SEO efforts can be complex, especially when dealing with long-term goals.

2 **Impact**: Difficulty in measuring ROI can lead to challenges in securing budget and stakeholder buy-in.

4. **Content Saturation and Competition:**

1. **Challenge**: The digital space is crowded with content, making it harder to stand out and capture audience attention.

2. **Impact**: High competition can reduce the effectiveness of content marketing and SEO efforts, leading to lower engagement and conversions.

5. **Balancing Quantity and Quality:**

1. **Challenge**: Striking the right balance between producing a high volume of content and maintaining its quality.

2. **Impact**: Prioritizing quantity over quality can harm brand reputation and user trust.

PRACTICAL SOLUTIONS AND BEST PRACTICES

1. Creating High-Quality Content Consistently:

1. **Solution**: Develop a content calendar to plan and schedule content in advance. Utilize a mix of content types (blogs, videos, infographics) to keep the audience engaged.

2. **Best Practice**: Invest in a dedicated content team or outsource to skilled content creators. Leverage user-generated content and guest contributions to diversify content sources.

2. Keeping Up with SEO Algorithm Changes:

1. **Solution**: Stay informed about algorithm updates through reputable SEO blogs, forums, and industry

news. Regularly audit and update your SEO strategy to align with the latest best practices.

2. **Best Practice**: Implement a flexible SEO strategy that can quickly adapt to changes. Focus on creating high-quality, user-focused content that aligns with search intent.

3. Measuring ROI:

1. **Solution**: Define clear goals and KPIs for content marketing and SEO efforts. Use analytics tools to track performance and attribute conversions to specific content and SEO activities.

2 **Best Practice**: Create detailed reports that highlight key metrics, insights, and actionable recommendations. Use a combination of quantitative and qualitative data to demonstrate value.

4. Content Saturation and Competition:

1. **Solution**: Conduct thorough competitor analysis to identify gaps and opportunities. Focus on niche topics and unique perspectives to differentiate your content.

2. **Best Practice**: Emphasize quality over quantity. Use data-driven insights to create content that addresses audience needs and solves specific problems.

5. Balancing Quantity and Quality:

1. **Solution**: Set realistic content production goals that prioritize quality. Implement a review and editing process to maintain content standards.

2. **Best Practice**: Encourage collaboration between content creators, SEO experts, and marketing teams to ensure content is both high-quality and optimized for search engines.

FUTURE TRENDS IN CONTENT MARKETING AND SEO

1. Voice Search Optimization:

1. **Trend**: With the rise of voice-activated devices, optimizing content for voice search is becoming increasingly important.

2. **Action**: Focus on natural language processing and long-tail keywords that align with voice search queries.

2. Artificial Intelligence and Machine Learning:

1. **Trend**: AI and machine learning are transforming content creation, personalization, and SEO.

2. **Action**: Leverage AI tools for content recommendations, predictive analytics, and automating routine SEO tasks.

3. Visual and Video Content:

1. **Trend**: Visual content, including videos and infographics, continues to dominate user engagement.

2. **Action:** Invest in high-quality visual content and optimize it for SEO to enhance visibility and engagement.

4. Mobile-First Indexing:

1. **Trend**: Search engines prioritize mobile-friendly websites in their indexing and ranking algorithms.

2. **Action**: Ensure your website is responsive, fast-loading, and optimized for mobile devices.

5. Personalization and User Experience:

1. **Trend**: Personalization and enhancing user experience are critical for engaging and retaining audiences.

2. **Action**: Use data to create personalized content experiences and focus on improving site usability and accessibility.

By understanding and addressing the common challenges in content marketing and SEO, leveraging best practices, and staying ahead of future trends, marketers can optimize their strategies for sustained success. In the final chapter, we will bring everything together, recap key points, provide final tips and recommendations, and encourage continued learning and experimentation.

CHAPTER 18

BRINGING IT ALL TOGETHER

As we wrap up our journey through the world of content marketing and SEO, it's time to bring together the key insights and strategies discussed in this book. This final chapter will recap the essential points, provide actionable tips and recommendations, and encourage you to continue learning and experimenting. Let's dive in.

Recap of Key Points

1. Understanding Content Marketing:

1. **Definition and Evolution**: Content marketing involves creating and sharing valuable content to attract and engage a target audience. It has evolved from simple blog posts to a multifaceted strategy encompassing various formats and channels.

2. **Key Benefits**: Building brand awareness, establishing authority, fostering relationships, and driving conversions.

3. **Types of Content Marketing**: Blogs, videos, infographics, podcasts, social media posts, and more.

2. Developing a Content Marketing Strategy:

1. **Setting Goals and Objectives****: Define clear, measurable goals aligned with your business objectives.

2. **Identifying Your Target Audience**: Understand your audience's needs, preferences, and behaviors.

3. **Content Marketing Funnel**: Guide potential customers through the stages of awareness, consideration, and decision-making.

3. Content Planning and Ideation:

1. **Topic Research and Ideation Techniques**: Use tools and methods to generate relevant and engaging content ideas.

2. **Creating a Content Calendar**: Plan and schedule your content to ensure consistency and alignment with your strategy.

3. **Types of Content Formats**: Explore various formats to diversify your content and cater to different audience preferences.

4. Creating High-Quality Content:

1. **Writing Compelling Blog Posts**: Craft informative and engaging blog posts with clear structure and compelling headlines.

2. **Crafting Engaging Videos**: Produce high-quality videos that capture attention and deliver value.

3. **Designing Infographics and Visuals**: Use visuals to simplify complex information and enhance engagement.

5. Introduction to SEO:

1. **What is SEO and Why It Matters**: SEO involves optimizing your content and website to rank higher in search engine results, driving organic traffic.

2. **How Search Engines Work**: Understand search engine algorithms and ranking factors.

3. **Key SEO Terms and Concepts**: Familiarize yourself with essential SEO terminology.

6. Keyword Research:

1. **Importance of Keyword Research**: Identify relevant keywords to optimize your content and improve search visibility.

2. **Tools for Keyword Research**: Utilize keyword research tools to discover high-potential keywords.

3. **Long-Tail vs. Short-Tail Keywords**: Balance between targeting broad and specific keywords.

7. On-Page SEO:

1. **Optimizing Titles and Meta Descriptions**: Craft effective titles and meta descriptions to improve click-through rates.

2 **Effective Use of Headers and Subheaders**: Structure your content with headers to enhance readability and SEO.

3. **Image Optimization and Alt Text**: Optimize images for faster loading times and better search visibility.

8. Technical SEO:

1. **Website Speed and Performance**: Ensure your website loads quickly to improve user experience and rankings.

2. **Mobile-Friendliness and Responsive Design**: Optimize your site for mobile users.

3. **XML Sitemaps and Robots.txt**: Use these tools to help search engines crawl and index your site efficiently.

9. Content Optimization for SEO:

1. **Writing SEO-Friendly Content**: Integrate keywords naturally and focus on quality.

2. **Incorporating Keywords Naturally**: Avoid keyword stuffing and prioritize readability.

3. **Content Length and Readability**: Balance content length with readability to keep readers engaged.

10. Link Building and Backlinks:

1. **Importance of Backlinks**: Build high-quality backlinks to improve your site's authority and rankings.

2. **Strategies for Acquiring Quality Backlinks**: Use methods like guest blogging and influencer outreach.

3. **Guest Blogging and Influencer Outreach**: Leverage external platforms and partnerships for backlinks and visibility.

11. Content Distribution and Promotion:

1. **Social Media Marketing**: Promote your content on social media to reach a broader audience.

2. **Email Marketing Campaigns**: Use email to distribute content and nurture leads.

3. **Paid Advertising**: Invest in paid campaigns to amplify your content reach.

12. Advanced SEO Techniques:

1. **Schema Markup and Structured Data**: Enhance your content with structured data to improve search visibility.

2. **Local SEO Strategies**: Optimize for local searches to attract nearby customers.

3. **Voice Search Optimization**: Adapt your content for voice search queries.

13. Content Marketing Automation:

1. **Tools for Automating Content Marketing**: Use automation tools to streamline content creation and distribution.

2. **Workflow Automation**: Automate repetitive tasks to save time and resources.

3. **Benefits and Challenges of Automation**: Understand the advantages and potential pitfalls of automation.

14. Analytics and Performance Measurement:

1. **Key Metrics to Track**: Monitor traffic, engagement, and conversion metrics.

2. **Tools for Monitoring and Analyzing Performance**: Utilize analytics tools to gain insights.

3. **Using Data to Refine Your Strategy**: Make data-driven decisions to optimize your efforts.

15. Successful Content Marketing and SEO Case Studies:

1. **Examples of Successful Campaigns**: Learn from real-world examples of effective content marketing and SEO.

2. **Lessons Learned from Top Brands**: Apply insights from leading brands to your strategy.

3. **How to Replicate Their Success**: Implement proven tactics to achieve similar results.

FINAL TIPS AND RECOMMENDATIONS

1. **Stay Informed and Adapt**: The digital marketing landscape is constantly evolving. Keep abreast on the most recent trends, algorithm modifications, and best practices. Continuously adapt your strategies to remain competitive.

2. **Prioritize User Experience**: Always focus on providing value to your audience. Provide educational, interesting, and user-friendly information. Prioritize website speed, mobile-friendliness, and easy navigation.

3. **Leverage Data and Analytics**: Use analytics tools to track performance, gain insights, and make data-driven decisions. Regularly review your metrics to identify areas for improvement and optimize your strategy.

4. **Experiment and Innovate**: Don't be afraid to try new approaches and experiment with different content formats, channels, and tactics. Innovation can set you apart from the competition and drive better results.

5. **Build Relationships and Collaborate**: Foster relationships with influencers, industry experts, and other brands. Collaborate on content, guest posts, and backlink opportunities to expand your reach and authority.

6. **Maintain Consistency**: Consistency is key in content marketing and SEO. Maintain a regular posting schedule, adhere to your brand voice, and ensure a consistent user experience across all touchpoints.

7. **Invest in Continuous Learning**: Digital marketing is a dynamic field. Invest in ongoing education, attend industry conferences, participate in webinars, and read authoritative blogs and books to enhance your knowledge and skills.

ENCOURAGEMENT FOR CONTINUED LEARNING AND EXPERIMENTATION

As you embark on your content marketing and SEO journey, remember that success doesn't happen overnight. It calls for commitment, perseverance, and a readiness to take lessons from both achievements and setbacks. Embrace the process of experimentation, and don't be discouraged by setbacks. Each challenge you encounter is an opportunity to learn, grow, and refine your strategy.

Stay curious and open to new ideas. The digital marketing landscape is filled with endless possibilities and opportunities for innovation. By continuously learning and adapting, you can stay ahead of the curve and achieve long-term success.

CONCLUSION

Content marketing and SEO are powerful tools that, when used effectively, can transform your digital presence and drive meaningful business results. This book has provided a comprehensive roadmap, from understanding the fundamentals to exploring advanced techniques and real-world case studies.

As you move forward, apply the insights and strategies shared in this book to your own efforts. Keep your audience at the heart of everything you do, prioritize quality and consistency, and leverage data to make informed decisions. Stay adaptable, be willing to experiment, and invest in continuous learning.

Your journey in content marketing and SEO is an ongoing one, filled with opportunities to innovate, engage, and grow. Accept the difficulties, rejoice in the successes, and never give up on your quest for greatness. With dedication and the right approach, you can achieve remarkable success and make a lasting impact in the digital world.

Thank you for joining me on this journey. Here's to your continued success in content marketing and SEO!

www.ingramcontent.com/pod-product-compliance
Lightning Source LLC
Chambersburg PA
CBHW071924210526
45479CB00002B/539